eBay
HOW TO EARN
£50,000
A YEAR
PART TIME

Work Full Time &
Earn Part Time then swap

ISBN 9781511813808

About the Author

My name is George Wallace I was born in Newport-on-Tay, Fife, Scotland. School was a disaster for me. At first, I was constantly told off for not writing down what was on the blackboard. My mum used to hate going to school in the evenings to hear all the complaints about me. Then a rather brilliant teacher took notice of me and asked my mother, "Have you had his eyes tested?" As it turned out, I was short-sighted and could not read the blackboard. Fixing this small but critical problem certainly improved the situation. After that, I quickly discovered another hidden quality about myself; I could run! It was only after finding running that things began to get better. Then, at age 15, I was informed by the Rector of my school (Bell Baxter Senior High School, in Cupar Fife) that I was never going to be anyone and was destined to fail all of my GCSEs. I decided to prove him totally wrong; however, one month later, I left school with no qualifications and little hope. But determined never to give up and to prove the Rector wrong.

Shortly after, I enlisted in the Royal Air Force and began my apprenticeship in 219 Entry at RAF Halton. It was great fun as I spent the next 12 years in the RAF working on the English Electric Lightning, the Jaguar, Buccaneer inflight refuelling system and testing Jaguar Jet Engines. In my final two years, I did a SCOTEC (equivalent to an ONC) in Electrical and Electronic Engineering. I was accepted for an Honours Degree in Electrical and Electronic Engineering at Dundee Institute of Technology, better known as Bell Street Tech.

I passed the program with a 2.1 and went on to join BAe at Brough, designing and building Hawks. They put me into production because I was one of the few people who knew what an aircraft looked like; in fact, it's somewhat worrisome that all of my colleagues were designing aircraft. I had worked on the starting system on the Jaguar for six years and, as a result, knew how it worked and the same one was used on the Hawk. Additionally, I knew the staff involved in the manufacture and design processes. I asked about working on it and was told that a friend, John, had worked on the system for three months and was getting on well. I got a job doing Systems Engineering, and I never looked back. I worked with a very demanding customer on a $1 billion programme leading a Systems Engineering Team. From that, I learnt how the Systems Engineering lifecycle works. I spent a lot of time agreeing with the customer what they actually wanted in reports. It made my life easier, and I learnt a great deal about negotiations and how to speak and deal with your customer.

I went to 3SL for nine months as a consultant, then on to Lockheed Martin working on Air Traffic Control Systems. Then, it was back to BAe to work on aircraft carriers, designing the aircraft systems to be integrated into the aircraft carriers. Finally, I ended up at Raytheon Systems, where after two short years my position was deemed redundant, the worst experience of my life. The redundancy was managed in the worst way possible, but it begs the question what is the best way to manage it.

Just before I was made redundant, I started an eBay account to sell some old items from a kitchen I had just built. My products sold all right and before I knew it, I was hooked. After the redundancy had been announced, I spent the next three months setting up an infrastructure to sell on eBay. Since then, I've kept the eBay business going while working on various contracts as an engineer.

Despite this, eBay has become an integral part of my life that I enjoy and find very rewarding.

Foreword

This is the story of my eBay store. I welcome new and returning customers every day to my shop on eBay, one of the world's largest e-commerce sites. I find that, like any guest, my visitors respond best to being welcomed with open arms. What I have found over the years is that Customers can be delighted and happy, or they can be in a dismal mood. No matter how good you are, you simply cannot please everyone all the time. But I have been at this for some time and continue to learn each day, either through my business itself or through research to better prepare myself for what my business may bring.

As a bit of background, I have been running my eBay-based business for over three years and have amassed more than 18000 feedbacks. It's been a steep learning curve and in this book, my goal is to share with you some of the experiences that I've had. In doing so, I hope to help you avoid making the mistakes that I have made. After all, the most important thing I've done has been to strive to only make each mistake once.

Through my experience, I have created this book as a guide that is designed to help you create and manage your very own eBay business and run it part time or full time. You could just as easily use this information to start any business, particularly in the world of e-commerce. After all, I've had lots of experiences—good and bad—that you can learn from before tackling your new endeavour.

In fact, the majority of what follows is great advice for any retail business. This book contains proven advice on how to start your business and make it a success. I'll start off with the simplest piece of wisdom a business owner will need:

- **You must make a profit on everything that you sell.**
- **If you don't make a profit, your business isn't going to be successful, and you may as well give up now.**

Other important aspects of a successful business include concentrating on the customers and providing excellent customer service. If you get it right, you will earn repeat customers and make a tidy profit (which is, key in owning a business). This is especially critical on eBay, where customers that experience problems with their orders expect to be treated poorly and receive a slow or no reply. By ensuring that you attend to all of your customer's needs, no matter how small, you can't go wrong. From there, find the right stock to sell, make a profit, and enjoy your well-deserved rewards.

With that in mind, please enjoy this book and use it to start your own business. And don't put it on the shelf—you're looking for **self**-development, not **shelf** development.

Contents

1

Introduction

The information in this book is a step-by-step guide to creating a successful eBay business that you can run part time. I have personally utilised these steps to create and manage my own eBay business while building up plenty of strong positive feedback and a solid rapport with my customers. In exchange, I've established a solid base of repeat customers, in addition to adding new buyers every day. So without further ado, let's get started! This is the model that I used when working part time on eBay and turning over £50,000 a year.

2

The First Step – Finding Stock

If I received one pound from everyone who asked the question, "Where do you get your stock from," I would be a millionaire. The first thing to remember is that where you get your stock from is your business and no one else's. Tell no one where you receive your stock from. Once you have decided what you want to sell on eBay, you have to find stock. Aunty Margaret's socks that she has been sending you for 20 years will not last forever. My advice is that do not attempt to purchase branded goods from China—and claim that they are authentic in your marketing. This will save you a lot of problems as buyers will very quickly find that they are not authentic. I purposely ordered some samples from China which were obviously fake. I knew this because the original manufacturer is not based in China just to have a look at them. They were awful. Some of the marketing on them was obviously not the real deal.

It is important that you do your homework and keep on looking to improve your stock constantly. It is really beneficial to be familiar with your stock since you will be asked questions about it. Once you have found what you want to sell as a serious business, have a look online and find out how similar items are selling on eBay and use Google to see what they are selling for. Work out whether or not they would be profitable. That is the most important thing you must do online or in any business: MAKE A PROFIT. If you are happy with the product, contact the vendor and ask for some samples. Do not go out and purchase hundreds of them. Once they arrive, examine them carefully and make sure that they are in first-class condition. Point of note, would you buy them? Always ask yourself that question.

Ask yourself this question: If someone buys this, what problem will it solve for them? This is a very important question since this is what your marketing is based on. Understanding a person's problem helps you to understand why they would buy it and, of course, why they would buy it from you.

Take foundation (makeup) for example most women are looking for great coverage and something that stays on all day. It makes you look beautiful, keeps you looking young. All of these are hooks that attract people to purchase. Everyone wants to look younger and more beautiful. Similarly, busy people do not want to have to keep on touching up their foundation all the time. This leads you to the next step: know your audience. Who is buying from you? Do not say everyone because that's simply not true. But it may be a cross section. Remember you may be selling foundation, but male and female customers could purchase it. Lots of men wear makeup these days. You want to aim your message at your main audience and adjust your description to get them to buy from you. I had a problem with a product and had to give refunds to the customers who bought it. But I learnt something from this experience—why they purchase the product and what they use it for. Once you have that under control, you have found the solution to the problem that you are solving. In any case, I was able to buy more stock and use the solution to help sell it. Sometimes a small mistake can lead to much bigger opportunities.

So put your few items on to eBay, taking your time to describe them. Take brilliant photographs that stand out from your competitors. Make sure your photographs are clear and meets the eBay standards. If possible, give your photographs a white background. It makes a massive difference and makes you look far more professional. Use all the room that you have for the title, and make it stand out.

When it comes to titles, here's another example. Would you look at "Ford Fiesta Blue 1973" or "Ford Fiesta 1973 Blue Full MOT 12000 miles only one careful owner"? The cars might be the same, but by putting a more descriptive title, you'll stand out to the audience thus making your item more attractive. Equally important, using key words means that your item will be found.

When setting the price make the standard posting free if possible, but adding charges for tracked mail. Add the charged option for Tracked Mail. Find out what it costs to post and add that cost to the value of your item. Tell your visitors to buy it now and they might just do it. It's called a call to action. Tick all the boxes and put it online. Some things sell instantly while others take time. I usually allow items to sit for about a week while people look at it. Go back every so often and check how many visitors have been to look at your item. If you have variants of the item, use the variation option in eBay. This results in more people looking at your products, plus it gives them more choice. They may buy one for themselves and one for their friend.

If your item starts selling like crazy, you have either found a great winner or you have set the price too low. Do your market research again to check what the price should be. I have sold dozens of items in a day, only to find that I had set the price too low.

If it does not sell at all, either it's not selling on eBay or something is wrong with it. Keep a watchful eye on the number of visitors to your page. Try changing the title to attract more customers. Also, check your price as it may be too high. Whatever you change, make the change then leave it. You want to see the effect it has. You need to leave things for around 48 hours to see if the change that you have made has had any effect. Do not make dozens of changes and find your item suddenly selling, since you have no idea which change caused it to start selling. It's like having a healthy condition and seeking treatment from different specialists at the same time. By using multiple remedies. You would struggle to pinpoint what actually cures you.

If you sell a few items and business is slow but steady, you have probably found the right formula. Just let your test run and find out what happens. It's really the only way to do it. You have run your tests, discovered the effect of a solid formula, and avoided spending a fortune on stock. If the item does not sell, then you have a few items to take to the next car boot sale to sell. If you had bought hundreds – well, you would have a problem on your hands with what to do with the extra stock. Extra stock takes up storage space and most important of all, the funding for more stock of the items that sell.

Assuming that the trial has been successful, go back to your supplier and re-order. The supplier will be hoping for a huge order. This time, go for around 24 items depending on how confident you are that they will sell again. If you are not confident, do not purchase too many and try selling again. If you are not happy with the sales performance of the item, do not buy in bulk. If you are happy with the sales performance then purchase as many as you are comfortable with. Do not forget to negotiate with the supplier for the best deal that you can get. You can tell them that you intend to extend the range and buy more next time. Always go for a lower price plus keep shopping around for a cheaper supplier.

I started with this supplier, and they told me that they would never drop prices. I stayed with the supplier for some considerable time, but I wanted to try to find another product that they did not sell. I went searching and found another supplier who sold what I wanted. Even better, I discovered that the new supplier was far cheaper and they offered a wider range of what I wanted plus they are more efficient. The first supplier was very shocked when I started putting in small orders. On asking why, I informed them about my new discovery. What was funny not only did they want to know who the new supplier was they also wanted to speak to me to offer me a discount on my subsequent orders. The lesson from my experience is that keep marketing for better suppliers and you will find them. You will then be amazed how quickly your current suppliers will want to provide goods at competitive prices – keep working hard to save money. If you buy from overseas (i.e. USA), remember you have to ship the items, and you have to pay the Customs charge on arrival in the UK or your home country. This can be expensive, and it takes time.

While waiting for new stock never put your new items onto eBay until your new stock has arrived. Items can get delayed and this leads to unhappy customers. When I first started getting my orders delivered by courier, I would receive an email stating that the order was due to arrive between noon and 1 p.m. At 12:15, another email would appear stating that I was not in. Yet I was sat waiting for the delivery and they never arrived. They claimed all sorts of rubbish but the reality was that they never turned up. Imagine if you had put the items that were in your order on eBay relying on the order being delivered. If any were sold you would be in trouble as there are no guarantees that the supplier will deliver the next day. Until they get to know you well.

The best place to find new suppliers is the British Library or Business Library. They both have brilliant lists of suppliers who are not on Goggle showing that they sell the products you are searching for. You can obtain their contact details directly and contact them. These are high-class suppliers, but you may have to purchase a minimum stock level, which you may not be able to afford or store. What you are looking for is a supplier who is receiving goods directly from the manufacturer or to purchase directly from the manufacturer yourself.

A few words of caution:

- Beware of purchasing stock that has a shelf life. You may find yourself with lots of useless stock that you cannot sell.
- Beware of people offering you discounted products and fantastic offers 'guaranteed to sell'. They normally do not sell. Plus you need to work the margins that you will receive in selling the article. I am often offered products, and on doing the market research find them to be selling on eBay for less than I am being asked to pay for them. My suggestion is stick with what you know and understand initially

3

Becoming a Power Seller on eBay

I have been a Power Seller on eBay for some years now. Despite all the efforts to obtain this status. I'm sad to report that this distinction is slated for removal from eBay. It has benefited my business tremendously so I will be very disappointed when it goes or is no longer accredited to exceptional sellers on eBay.

When you first start selling a few household items on eBay, it seems so easy and there's no real pressure. Every sale brings a thrill. Then, after a short time, you move to the crucial step of making the decision to go for it and turn your eBay account into a business—that's when the real fun begins.

First, you need to find stock to sell. When you are looking for items and get offered a great deal by a wholesaler, take it easy and be sure to only purchase a few things. The wholesaler will be offering you all sorts of incentives to buy additional stock. Ignore these deals and just buy the minimum that you can purchase, about three items or so. If the cost is high, try to negotiate for a lower price with the promise of future orders. After all, when you're just starting out, money can be tight and it's important that you minimise your start-up costs. If you look after the pennies, the pounds will look after themselves.

After you've received your product, list the three items and wait for them to sell. Before pricing the items, be sure to do some market research and figure out what the items are being sold for on eBay and other e-commerce sites. Ignore the items that are being sold via auction—the prices are sometimes very low or very high, but it's almost always difficult to determine the correct price. However, you can certainly take note of the prices that these auctions finish at.

If you're new to eBay, you want to place your item at the middle-to-upper end of the price range. Be sure not to list your item at the lowest price possible. If your item (or similar items) isn't already on eBay, go for a price that will make you a profit. In fact, make sure that no matter what you do, you always make a profit. It's also worthwhile to check out products on Google and find out what they're priced at.

I recently checked the price of a laptop that I had purchased for £307. The highest price was £510, meaning that the range was about £200. Shopping around on Google takes mere minutes and can save you hundreds of pounds.

Next up is creating a title for your item. You'll want to start with the manufacturer and the product. Then add in marketing words, like "anti-ageing," making sure that you use keywords in the title. Whatever you use, make sure that you use as many of the 80 characters as you can. Make the photograph unique for your item, using your imagination to create something different and appealing.

The description is a great place to welcome people into your shop. Then provide a great description of how the item will solve their problem. Use a call to action and be sure to ask them to come back again. Over time, you'll start to develop a template that works well as you gain more experience. It took me in the region of three years to get to a template that I liked and worked to my satisfaction. Even now, I am still tweaking it to make improvements. It is always helpful to listen to your customers, and if they comment on your item, take note. For instance I made a mistake by not changing the title and description of an item which ran out of stock. I purchased new stock not realising that it was slightly different to the original product. The customers started complaining that the product was not correct and they provided explanation as to why. This however was vital information as I used it in marketing the product. I updated the product description with the marketing information which significantly increased my sales.

Then, set your price. If you set it too low, you risk not being able to raise it and keep your sales going. Set it too high, and you'll risk not selling the item. You have to find a middle ground. But remember, your aim on eBay is to make a profit. When you calculate the price of items, you have to take into account: theft, postal loss, refunds, and transaction fees (from eBay and PayPal). Once you figure out these numbers, you can make sure that every sale will yield a profit.

Next, always keep a watch on the number of viewers to find out how popular your item is. If you aren't getting any viewers, do some research and check out similar products. Plus, check for items that have sold and determine if there is a trend causing them to sell.

Now that you have your three items listed, there are several possible scenarios:

1. All three items sell very quickly—this is a popular product; buy more stock and put it on eBay. This

time, raise the price slightly. Keep doing this as long as the item sells.

2.   One item sells and the other two do not—take a look at the title, description and check how many views you are getting.

3.   Nothing sells—check how many viewers you have and if you have any watchers. Do some more research and check your price compared with other items on sale. Check the spelling of the title and consider revising the description.

In some cases, I have found a title that wasn't great and checked out the keywords. I changed the title and description around, only to find sales take off! This has happened a few times and is easy to fix. The other problem can be spelling. If your title has a critical spelling mistake in it no one will find it. For instance selling a Foord Feista. There is no Ford car by that name so you will attract no real buyers. What you will attract is a type of smart buyer looking for spelling mistakes to make a profit from you.

Once you determine the best price and description to start getting you sales, then start to purchase more stock. Increase your stock levels by small amounts. Once three are sold, go for six and then twelve. If they continue to sell, then go for the higher numbers. But remember that when you purchase stock, you are spending your capital, so unless you are absolutely sure, do not tie too much capital in the stock. If the item does not sell have a play about with it, but do not invest in more stock if it still is not selling. One caution, though, is to beware of holding too much stock and running out of capital. It is easy to do.

Another thing to beware of is the "sell by date" of the product if you're buying something that expires. You may purchase 1000 bottles of a product only to find out that after 18 months it is unusable. For instance, most fake tanning products turn green after 18 months. You will get lots of upset customers with green tans and will be left with stock that is unusable.

Now that your sales on eBay are starting to grow it is guaranteed that you will receive questions about orders or your products. Get into the habit of replying to questions as quickly as possible and you begin to build a reputation. This will delight your customers since they do not expect to receive a reply for at least two or three days if at all. Your effective response would reassure the Customer that you are a professional eBay seller. When a customer has asked for a refund or you have agreed to give a refund, provide the refund immediately. Do not wait for two or three days. Providing it immediately reduces the risk of receiving a negative feedback for an item not received or a problem left unresolved.

Some customers will sit at their device and reply immediately. Beware of this as you can easily get sucked into conversations that can go on for ages. When you receive an immediate reply, do not reply straight away. At the same time be aware of the buyer who will not respond to your response.

Even Customers who respond, some of them can be quite challenging and uncooperative. Totally ignoring your question and constantly stating "my order has not arrived". One Customer claimed that they had only received one item and they refused to send a photograph of the envelope, where the coded number of items can be found. In such cases, ask for the order to be returned and inform the Customer that a full refund would be provided once the returned item has been received.

Once you begin to receive more feedback, you become more prominent on eBay, and your products will move further up in eBay and Google rankings as your performance improves.

4

Finding an Accountant

One of the first steps to take when starting your eBay business is to find a good accountant. You are going to require their services at the end of each year, so it's important that you find one whom you can trust. In all honesty, you should do this before you file to incorporate as a business.

You'll also need to establish an automated process to manage each transaction, in order to capture your sales from PayPal. Assuming you are selling an average of ten items per day, at the end of the year, you'll have over 3500 transactions to account for. Even with relatively low sales, it can be difficult to keep track of everything manually. You'll have your payments and invoices for stock and other bills. Taking all of these into account, the number of transactions you deal with annually may even exceed 4000!

In these times of austerity, governments (worldwide) are doing their best to extract as much extra money from their citizens as possible, so they'll take advantage of any excuse to issue a fine. Therefore, it's incredibly important to be meticulous in your accounting.

That's why your first step is to find an accountant you can trust. A poor or untrustworthy accountant can cause you huge problems, particularly if they submit incorrect final accounts. My business has experienced this and it wasn't pleasant. Use whatever means you wish to find someone, but make sure they have some knowledge of e-commerce. I sent out an e-mail request via a website and interviewed each of the accountants that applied. Better yet, try to get a referral from a friend or colleague that would recommend their accountant's services.

Once you've selected an accountant, sit down and talk to them about your business. Chances are that they are they will be knowledgeable about accounting, but the majority won't understand your new e-commerce business nor do they understand eBay. This is a mistake that lots of businesses make—assuming that banks, accountants, and other financial professionals that support you have an understanding of what you do but they don't.

A banker I recently met left school at 18 and went to university, then joined a bank as a small business specialist. He has never run a small business (and would likely run away from the amount of effort required!). I asked about opening an account and was told that I should put £200 into the account immediately; I would then be able to withdraw it again after seven days. Being somewhat puzzled by this, I investigated further. I discovered that it was a way to ensure that they received their bonus for opening the account. Personally, I don't believe this method of enrolling customers, in order to ensure a bonus for the banker, is an unethical business practice.

Unfortunately, another thing you'll have to do is guess what the future will hold. You'll need to estimate your turnover for the first year; this is what your accountant will base their fees on. I guessed low, unsure of how successful I was going to be. In fact, most people underestimate their performance for their first year in business. Regardless, be sure to agree on a set amount for your fees with your accountant. I agreed to an amount that would most likely be my turnover and doubled it. As a result, in the middle of the year, I was asked to pay additional fees. Needless to say, I learned the importance of negotiating my fees for the entire year upfront.

Being an eBay seller you will be familiar with PayPal. To track all your payments in PayPal, you'll need an application that links to PayPal and automatically records the data from each sale. Manually entering the estimated 3500+ transactions would be a lot of work, and you're almost guaranteed to make a few mistakes. But once you have the correct application in place your accounting package will record every transaction for you along with the name and details of the buyer. This part is critical and needs to work properly for every transaction. Thankfully, setting up the link to PayPal is relatively simple and, once you get used to it, you'll quickly become an expert in using this type of tool.

Once you start to get PayPal entries coming in, be sure to carry out an audit of your sales so far, to ensure that you are receiving every payment. It's important to keep your accounting package up to date, and when you receive your bank statement, check it against your accounting package. Ensure that the balance in your accounting package is the same as in your actual bank accounts. Once you've finished updating the bank statement, carry out the reconciliation between the two. When I move money from PayPal to my bank account, I add the details in my KashFlow account. It saves so much time when I am checking between the bank statements and the online account. It also lets me see how I am doing in the business.

As a quick note of advice (from personal experience), if your accounting package gets out of step with the bank statement, be sure to fix the problem immediately. My first accountant messed up my accounting package and the balances from the bank were miles out from my PayPal balance. Accountants will often make small adjustments to these accounting packages (not maliciously, of course) that lead to the accounts getting out of sync. If they do, be sure to have your accountant fix it and check in with them regularly until the numbers line up.

Once you've got everything through the first month of your accounting package, get your accountant to check that everything is in order and no problems exist with the data entry. If it isn't right, partner with your accountant to sort out the problem. Fixing one month's worth of data is relatively simple; doing it after 12 months is a total nightmare. The three years that I had to do were a marathon. You would not wish to be in the same position I was. Make sure to check on your accounts monthly, to ensure that you and your accountant can confidently and easily run your final accounts at the end of each financial year without any difficulties.

Checking these items regularly yourself is essential. My old accountant completely wrecked the data in my accounting package and left hundreds of mistakes over the course of three years. When the bank balances are the same, entering and checking your balances is a relatively simple task. But when the balances are not the same, it is easy to make mistakes since you have no way of validating the entries. It took me hours to fix the problems with my accounts after years of using an incompetent accountant. Nonetheless, it paid off in the end when all of my numbers finally lined up!

As a side note, some accountants will ask you to run your own accounting package. The benefit to this is that you have complete control. It is critical that you understand how to utilise the entirety of the accounting package. The accountant can help you to make sure that the account is running properly. However make sure that the accountant understands the package that you are using and can use it competently. If they cannot do this, you will end up with such a mess, and they will claim that the accounting package has problems itself.

Additionally, your accountant can be very helpful and provide excellent advice on certain financial matters. In your accounting package, there will be graphs that illustrate your business's performance. When I was relying fully on my accountant, the graphs never meant anything to me. But now that I am more involved in the financial reporting, I can see exactly how I am doing at a glance. This information is also great for spotting trends to help in making investment decisions.

My adventure with my first accountant wasn't exactly pleasant, but it made for a great early education, and I am happy to share it.

I would be requested to supply information by my accountant; efficient as I am, I would send it back very quickly. About a month later, I'd receive a phone call requesting the same information. At the end of the first year the accounts were in a mess. Although they were sorted out to balance at the end of the year, the figures never the less were miles out this caused a lot of unpredictable problems. Firstly it was impossible to deal with the accounts since the bank balance was miles out and the PayPal account was light years out.

When you entered the figures, you had no reference to work to. Therefore it was easy to make mistakes. Throughout the year, each time I entered the details, the PayPal and the bank balances were getting worse and worse. Worst of all the Accountant had informed the tax authority's things that I am still finding out about and trying to fix. Finally, at the end of the year, the final accounts had a massive loss. I was so fed up with the accountant. In consultation with my wife I simply accepted it. As I later found out this was a huge mistake, and I wish I had questioned it.

On checking my accounting system, I found that the accountant had essentially not used the accounting package to gather the figures and had instead made them up. On running the final accounts in the accounting package, I later found that the loss had, in fact, been about 1% of what had been reported. For these mistaken final accounts, I was charged additional fees, which I refused to pay. The accountant locked the accounting package and they essentially held me to ransom until I paid them. It was a long and tiresome battle to sort out my accounts. Meanwhile the accountant pretended everything was fine, leaving me to pick up the pieces. I wasted hundreds of hours fixing the work of the incompetent accountant and had to provide proof to various organisations based on the data provided. The accountant was chartered, so I thought they would work to a high standard, but that certainly wasn't the case.

I complained to the regulator about the accountant, but they seemed to be favourable to the accountant. In this situation it is important to remember that the accountant pays a professional membership fee to the regulator. Therefore I will leave you to draw your own conclusions.

On scrutinizing the accounts further I found huge errors in my accounts that were basically ignored by the regulator. Really and truly, you are on your own. The best advice I can give you is to find a good accountant who understands the accounting package you are using and work with them.

The second accountant did not know how to use the accounting package I was using. They claimed that they understood my accounting package but it became obvious that they did not have much of a clue. They came up with a lame excuse for not carrying on. But of course they will never admit it. Hopefully, the third one will be better.

The one thing that you are aiming to do on eBay is to make a profit. That should always be your ultimate goal. With a good accountant and by using the other techniques I am going to show you, this is very achievable. It's good fun and of course, not all accountants are bad and incompetent.

5

Customer Service on eBay

You can find the best deals with the potential to make a fortune on eBay. You can read all of these "expert" websites and have looked at the claims they make. But what they do not tell you is how to actually sell your items and provide good customer service.

There are two essential components of your business:

1. Put your items on eBay, get the attention of buyers, and sell your products.
2. Provide brilliant customer service.

Getting an item on to eBay is relatively simple; however, you must bear in mind that you have two great marketing tools for each item. First, the picture. The majority of sellers take boring pictures and put them on to eBay. It's of one item and it looks lonely and because the majority of other people do the same thing, it does not stand out. Take a photograph of 5 items all lined up, or in some other combination, but make your picture unique. You want your item to stand out from the crowd.

In the title, you have 80 characters to inform your potential buyer about your product. Use as many of the characters as you can. Tell them what the item is called, what it can do for them, and anything you are offering like free postage. Using the word "free" often has an amazing effect.

You load your great looking product onto eBay and it sells. Now after this, the process can be ridiculously easy or unnecessarily hard. First off, the item may get bought and not paid for. The buyer may have wanted to pay by PayPal and pressed another selection. In their infinite wisdom, eBay removed the ability to go back to "Pay by PayPal," causing innumerable problems. eBay do not allow you to send email addresses in their eBay emails. From this point forward, it's time for great customer service.

You receive an email saying that the customer wants to pay by PayPal, so you ask for their PayPal email address so you can send a request for payment. You start by asking, "Is your PayPal email address the same as your eBay email address?" Normally it is, so the problem is solved. However there are situations where this is not the case.

I regularly receive addresses that are missing data. Important things like a postcode. The most amusing post code I have come across is RACHEL12. Get back to the buyer and ask them to confirm their address. The number of mistakes that you find is amazing. But please take note if you send an order to an incorrect address it can cause you all sorts of problems. There is an offer that eBay makes to send items to Argos stores to permit the buyer to collect their order. You would be amazed at how Customers can confuse addresses, including their own. One Customer sent me the wrong address. Instead of providing the Argos address as per their choice, they provided the address of Boots which was next door to Argos - it caused so many problems. You then have to get your products back again and sort out with the Customer how they wish to proceed.

Sometimes, you get the email stating that they have not received their order. Emails in capital letters (signifying shouting—probably means they're angry) "WHERE IS MY ORDER" are your worst nightmare. You then write back, reminding them about the email that you sent the day the order arrived. I have had negative feedback from customers claiming that I do not reply to their emails and I have not sent their order. When the reality is they had written to me twice asking where their order was, only to ignore my email in reply asking them which address to send the item to. Nowadays, there is an address that is considered the address that you should post to by eBay. I have had the correct address on PayPal, the address on eBay and then a completely different address to ship to. If you mess up, it's important to remember it's you who gets the negative feedback, which eBay will not take off because the customer has not received their order.

The next potential customer issue takes a little longer to occur. It usually takes about two weeks after the item has been posted then an email arrives - the customer states that the item is either not as described or not received. This is where the problems may start. First, do you believe them? You can receive so many claims about eBay items that it's hard to believe anyone. I have had people claiming that they are disabled and never leave their bed. Only two days later, they email claiming to have been to a shop and been informed that the item is fake and that they want to report me to the manufacturer for sending out fake goods. These people who are trying to receive free products on eBay have a lot to answer for. With that in mind, despite all the goodwill in the world, don't believe anyone without evidence. Always ask for proof and wait until you receive it.

If an item has not arrived, I have a template that I send back that informs the buyer of the destination and the date their order was posted. This saves time. You either hear nothing back again or you get a note stating that the address is correct. Then it either goes very quiet or you get many emails. One very important thing to note: the postal systems in a majority of countries operate a system where they send out orders from a Distribution Centre. This is where you have to direct the buyer. Going to the Post Office is useless since they quite simply tell everyone that all mail has been delivered. I regularly receive packages returned from Distribution Centres stating "Not Collected." In the meantime, I am still receiving emails informing me that they have been to the Distribution Centre. Therefore advising your Customers to check at their local distribution office may help. However there are these Customers who are either not interested, can't be bothered or too lazy to check.

On receiving an email from a Customer about an item "not being as described," the first thing you want is photographic evidence. In this scenario expect a lot to happen - it either turns up instantly, you never hear from them again or you get a lot of abuse. The main problem have come across is customers buying multiple items from different sellers.

The other big problem has been a customer ordering more than one item and then claiming to have received the wrong number of items. To get around this, first use different colour tape on parcels with more than one item. Code the number of items into the order. When the claim arrives that only one item was sent instead of two, simply ask for a photograph of the envelope. At this point, it either goes very quiet or back comes the claim that they have thrown it in the bin. It is human nature to keep the envelope if one receives a parcel with the wrong number of items in it or another problem. However some customers really take the biscuit. Since I started using a coding system, the number of claims of "has not received the correct number of items" has just about disappeared.

As you can see, it's all about customer service. You will deal with all sorts of polite, rude, demanding, threatening and blackmailing customers. The blackmail is on the lines of, "If you do not give me a refund, I will give you negative feedback." One customer wrote to me claiming that the batch number on the product showed that it was out of date. They demanded a refund and they were not going to send the item back. I replied that if they required a refund then they should return the item. I also reported the person to eBay. Back came an email stating that they were not going to send the item back. They wanted a refund, and unless I gave it to them they were going to open a case against me and give me negative feedback for selling out of date stock. I contacted eBay once again, and they were reported again to Trust & Safety. I was advised to encourage the Customer to open a case since they would be requested to return the item to me with tracking that they pay for. This is called negative feedback extortion, along the lines of, "If you do not do what I want I am going to give you negative feedback." In most of these cases, eBay will take the negative feedback off.

Customer satisfaction also varies widely. One person that I helped was very happy, and I received orders from most of the street that they lived in.

You would be surprised to know that some countries are very difficult to sell to. I blocked one country because I had so many claims about items not being received. I received an email the next day that said, "I have bought lots of items from you and would like to keep on using you." I checked them out, and they had never bought anything from me and of course I will never know what their motives were.

One of the biggest problems that I have had recently was a person in a Rest of the World country. They claimed that they had received the wrong item and wanted a replacement sent. I sent an email asking for a photograph. They refused. Then it dawned on me: I had posted the item a day before and it takes at least five working days to arrive. Every email that I sent was replied to with abuse. I contacted eBay and spoke to a very helpful person. EBay investigated the claim and, to give them time, I informed the buyer that I was consulting with eBay about their case. The case remained open for about 10 minutes and was closed by the Customer.

The most important thing about customer service is to keep the customer informed at all times of any problems and make sure that all correspondence is on eBay since you may need that later as evidence. If they give you negative feedback, it is possible to have it removed as long as you can prove that you did everything correct. It is therefore vital to keep all emails in the eBay system to retain the evidence of what you have done to resolve the issue.

The rules for removing feedback keep on changing, thus I am not going to give any further advice on this subject.

6

Managing your eBay Account

You have registered on eBay as a business. This is the first step on the road to being successful. Your turnover on eBay is going to increase greatly if you get it right. Your eBay fees are going to rise; due to more sales but the costs that eBay charges for each sale falls significantly. Typically as a private seller eBay charges you an amount for each listing. However on becoming a business seller the typical fee for listing becomes free or significantly less. The first thing you should do is to set up eBay so that PayPal pays the eBay fees monthly. This is simple to do, but now you have to manage your PayPal account so that you retain enough balance to pay your eBay fees.

There are two things to note: first, you will be billed for the month around the 20th. Also, you will see that your balance on your eBay account will drop around the 1st of the month—when you are calculating the fees you owe, always remember to add on the amount outstanding. Your balance is paid around the 1st of the month. After that, you're all set until the next month. Your bill may be for £500. But at the end of the month, due to other sales, your eBay balance may be around £950. This is why you have to keep a view on the total balance.

Whenever you update any item on eBay, it will show you the balance of the fees that you owe. Make sure when you transfer your PayPal balance to your bank account that you know what you owe in eBay fees.

Customers sometimes purchase an item and do not pay for it. This will go into your awaiting payment section. Keep a watchful eye on these items since they will go to a state where you can open a case against the buyer for not paying. Open the case when you are allowed to. Some customers get very upset because you have opened a case against them. I have had all sorts of complaints and threatening emails about this. It would seem that most customers feel that you shouldn't open a case against them; however, they will open a case very quickly against you. As soon as you open a case, most people pay for the item very quickly. On opening ten cases, I would say most often six people will pay. Make sure that you send the correct number of items they have ordered since it is very easy, especially if you are very busy to miss out on what they have ordered and send only one instead of what they ordered.

Customers will get in contact with you. What they often do is to order two items through but only purchase one with PayPal. When you send them an invoice for the item not paid for, they may ignore it until eBay starts to contact them about the case that you have just opened. Then you get an email complaining that they have been contacted by eBay. On checking, you will find a case open in the Resolution Centre. What you have to do is close the case and then cancel the order. Contact the buyer and ask them to accept the email that you have just received to cancel the order. Do not tell them that you have already cancelled the order or they will never accept the email. When they accept the email, you get your fees back. It may only be a small amount of money, but when taking 300 outstanding items into account, the amount that it costs your company adds up quickly.

As soon as the Request Final Value option appears, select it to get a refund of your final value fees. Letting items sit unsold is fine, but as soon as it is sold, eBay takes a final value fee for the sale. Make sure that you get a refund of your fees if the customer has not paid.

Some people seem to get a buzz out of ordering things and not paying for them. I regularly receive orders for items that have not been paid for. This leaves you in a dilemma do you put it back on the shelf or do you wait for a payment that may never arrive. This is a challenge since if you put them back on to eBay and then the original order gets paid, you may run out of stock. Normally at this point I report them to eBay and block them. But wait until the refund is provided for the final value fee before relisting your items. It makes it difficult to manage your stock like this. It is easier to set the option that every order must be paid for by PayPal. It makes your stock far easier to manage than having to check stock values continually.

When a buyer causes you any problems, contact eBay and file a report with Trust and Safety. Using the pull-down menu in the sold section, report the buyer. This may seem like overkill, but its how you build up a history against a person who may constantly be claiming that items have not arrived. Always check to see if the person asking the question is a seller on eBay. I have found some very interesting sellers claiming not to have received their order that have lots of negative feedback. Then the aim seems to be to attempt to give you negative feedback, in an effort to hurt their competition—you! I have had cases closed and negative feedback removed just because I take a few minutes to report the customer. One person opened cases against me for items not received. They had sent me lots of emails asking where I obtained my stock from. I obviously did not provide them with that information.

I have had claims of items not received where I reported the customers to eBay, and they were banned within a few hours. You can tell that this happened when an email turns up informing you that this user ID is no longer trading on eBay.

I have multiple methods of paying for orders. eBay owns PayPal at the moment so that is the main payment method used. When a customer chooses to pay by another method, you send them an email asking how they would like to pay. Do this immediately after they have ordered, or you find your stock levels going down on eBay, and you can do nothing about it until you have cancelled your order. One customer, who was new to eBay, ordered ten individual items but paid for none. I eventually guided them how to cancel their orders. Helping customers' gives you job satisfaction plus it delights the customer that they are receiving the attention that they crave.

When customers discover all the steps they have to go through to pay by other means, they suddenly want to pay by PayPal. Unfortunately, they then discover that eBay removed the ability to go back to pay by PayPal once they initially rejected it.Being good at customer service, you, of course, offer to provide a payment via PayPal. The first thing that you have to find out is what the email address of their PayPal account is. This sounds really simple isn't it, but it may not be. You cannot send your e-mail address in an eBay message. However you can send a message that asks if their eBay e-mail is the same as their PayPal e-mail address. It's interesting here since sometimes you receive an email in an eBay message with their PayPal email address included. Other times, I have had a message with the Customer's email address cunningly split up into three parts—put it together, and you can work it out. Once it comes back, send them a PayPal request for payment. They normally pay quite quickly. Then post the order. You'll want to go back after and cancel the order in eBay. This is because you cannot link the individual payment in PayPal with the order. If you do not cancel the eBay order you may inadvertently open up a case against the Customer due to non-payment.

Paying by cheque or bank transfer is sometimes a huge problem. Customers ask to pay this way and then get bogged down in details. All your payment processor requires is the account and sort code details. Banks do their best to take their huge cut out of everything you pay into your account. The worst experience was a postal order for £10, where the bank wanted to charge £7. I paid the fee and went to see my Relationship Manager at the bank, who refunded the charges. What a lot of hassle for £7.

Having all these details at hand makes life very easy, especially if you can just cut and paste your bank account details into an email. The BIC and IBAN codes that overseas banks ask for contain the account and sort code details. So why you then get asked for sort code and account number as well is beyond me.

I am regularly asked if customers can purchase my stock in bulk at a discount. This sound great doesn't it, but remember that if your margins are quite small, then you could end up losing money on your bottom line. Plus, when you receive a request for a discount, you can take quite a lot of time listing all your stock and working out discounts only to send it off and receive no reply. The best way is to get the customer to list what they want and how much they are prepared to pay, based on your listed price. Please not that some Customers come up with rather low offers and when you refuse to sell at that price they can get upset about it. This whole process can be time consuming, but with the right offer it would make you a substantial profit

Remember one thing here - postage costs. A customer quotes £4 each and you think that's a great price. Then you have 20 to post and a high postage cost for a heavy parcel. The prices that customers come back with are often very low, and there is no way that you would make any profit with what they are quoting. The best way to deal with this is to go back and make a counteroffer with a price that will make you a profit. I have also had customers who have requested to buy in bulk many times. I have sent off PayPal requests for payment and never heard a thing until they come back wanting the next order.

Once you are starting to sell, it's time to open a shop on eBay. This is a simple process. Follow it through, and use the basic shop to start with. I have stayed with the basic shop since I started. There are offers available to provide just about every gadget going.

Finally, when it comes to managing your account, stick with the saying KISS—Keep it Simple Stupid. Customers are looking for things to solve problems. Make it simple and clear about what it is that you are offering, and put it straight in front of their face. You have about six seconds of a person's attention span for them to make up their mind. Your item may look great with branding and displays, but that is not what you are selling. You have to put the item literally in the person's face when they open up your page. Why do you think that big organisations pay eBay to advertise their similar products at the top of your page? It's in your face as soon as you open the page. You might just click on one of their links. By making sure that your customers see your product quickly and clearly, you're on the right track to selling more.

7

Online Shoplifting

Stores have an infrastructure in place to police their stores with cameras, security guards and store detectives. The only way to nearly make it fool proof is to send everything by registered post fully tracked. Only problem is your prices go up astronomically. Even then, tracking has limitations due for example to the postal provider not scanning the order.

Some subjects are so complex that I could write a book about and am going to. Theft and fraud on eBay has reduced significantly from what it was. The problem is that some customers do not tell the truth, and it gets to a point where sellers find it hard to believe anyone. When this happens the same questions comes up every time: "The post office has to have a tracking number to find my order." The truth is they do not require one and if you have not paid for a tracking number, your package won't have one. Once you become more experienced on eBay, you will start to know who is telling the truth. However you may still come across some surprises. When this happens as I have found out through experience I am afraid the same questions will appear and there are two potential problems when it comes to loss and theft.

First, the Postal Provider can leave you with problems by not accurately delivering orders. Not leaving a card when the order will not fit through the letterbox or delivering the mail to the wrong address are fairly common occurrences. I experience this regularly at home and in my business. Plus, there are many stories in the media. For example one mail company dumping mail in the river and in bins rather than delivering it. There has been another story of all the mail for the street being put through the letterbox of the first house.

Then you have the person who is not telling the truth when they contact you. They come up with all sorts of stories about their order. However you have to deal with people on a case-by-case basis rather than generalising. I have a rule that for any order over a certain amount, is sent by registered post. Never the less I still regularly receive emails from customers asking what the tracking number is, only to discover when checking that the tracking number is not on the Royal Mail Track and Trace system. On Contacting Royal Mail I confirm that it's not in the system. Then you are informed that your package has probably not been scanned, but it will be okay. At this point, you've paid for the service, and they have failed you. On the other hand Royal Mail policy is that as a seller you have to wait 28 days to put in a claim and then at least 90 days to receive a refund, if ever. Then you get the statement that I dislike the most - "We are very sorry." Whenever a big corporation does this, it is the sorry statement that is often said with no compassion. It is single-handedly the statement that annoys me the most.

Then you face other challenges. To give you the best idea, I will provide some examples of my experiences:

- I had an eBay case raised recently about an item not received, and the customer wanted a refund. I sent an email back requesting that the buyer confirm their address and they told me that they had checked at the local distribution office on Friday, and the order was not there. That sounds like a perfectly good reply the only trouble was Friday was a Bank Holiday. I replied informing them it was a Bank Holiday on Friday. The reply came back, "I meant Thursday." But the damage had been done. I sent the email to them at 17:30 on Friday at this point, you just report them to eBay. Nothing that they say to you is believable since they have already not told the truth. I receive emails from customers claiming not to have received orders. If you are a seller processing a lot of orders a day it is inevitable that you will receive questions too. The best way to show professionalism is to respond to every question. Once you respond promptly the majority of problems will vanish, and you will never hear from them again. The trick is to show that you are highly organised.

- Each time that you receive claims for a problem with an order request photographic evidence. An example is an order I posted abroad on the 10th of the month. The buyer opened an eBay case claiming that I had sent an incorrect item and they requested a replacement item. I contacted the buyer and requested photographic evidence - they refused. Then I suddenly realised that today's date was the 12th just 2 days after the item had been dispatched. It takes a minimum of 5 working days for mail to reach that particular country. I attempted to explain how they couldn't have received their order, but this invited more abuse. I contacted eBay and were forwarded to the United States since this country's eBay platform falls under eBay.com. I tried to explain to someone from the US that it took 5 days to post from UK to the other country, but they did not understand. I contacted the UK eBay based in Dublin and explained. They wanted to investigate. This nice person requested that I put off my buyer for 24 hours. I did this and got back to them the next day. I informed them that I had contacted eBay, and I was waiting for a response. The eBay case was shut instantly. This demonstrates the amount of patience and professionalism required to deal with some eBay customers who clearly have an agenda.

- I used to sell this expensive range of product that caused me more problems than it was worth. I would constantly receive claims of fake, not received and not as described. One particular case where I learnt a harsh lesson sticks in my mind. It was after this that I found it difficult to believe anyone. I sent out an order to another European country. The customer received my order and claimed that one of the items was 'very hard and unusable'. I replied to the buyer and requested that they return it to me. They replied saying that they were disabled and had to stay in bed and could not go to the Post Office to send it back. Being kind, I sent a replacement item. They replied two weeks later. "Thank you for sending the replacement. I have been to the local supplier, who informed me that your items are fake. If you do not provide me with a full refund, I am going to give you negative feedback." The obvious question here is where was the person who was bedridden from the first response? Situations like these make it hard to believe anyone who contacts me. I contacted eBay, and the problem was sorted out. I have become hardened to these stories, but many other sellers have their businesses wrecked by these types of people. This person did me a huge favour by making me resistant to such stories - I now ask for proof with every claim. After all you can't buy an item from a High Street shop and the go back and claim all sorts, request a refund or else without evidence. It would not wash, better still the police could be called.

- To give another example with an expensive product, I received an email that stated, "I am going to send all of your products to the main laboratory of the manufacturer to prove that they are fake. I want a refund." I replied, "Thank you for your email. I look forward to hearing back from you when you receive the report." I never heard another word from the person. But if customers are making a career out of doing this, then they must be getting some sellers to provide them with refunds.

- I stopped sending orders to one country since I was having cases opened regularly that claimed they had not received their order that I had sent weeks ago. When I stopped sending to this country, I received lots of emails from people pleading that I continue selling to them. But I was spending hours replying to people who just wanted their money back. You would post an item on 10th January. The customer would contact me on 20th March claiming their order had not arrived.

- I would receive cases that stated the item is not as described. I would respond by requesting that the buyer returned the item for a refund. But I did not receive any items returned and never heard again from any of the buyers. One buyer contacted me and demanded that I pay the postage since it was about £10 to send back the product by registered post. I agreed and never heard another thing. I did not pay and no more was heard.

• The biggest scam going on at present is dishonest customers who open eBay cases and claim not to have received their order. Worst of all you respond to the buyer and don't receive any reply. The buyer then waits for 7 days and contacts eBay to resolve the claim. It puts you in a very difficult position—do you provide a refund or wait it out? When eBay processes the majority of claims for buyers that haven't received their item, the customer often wins the case.

• One good point to note though is that when a customer opens a case against you and raises the case to eBay, you can immediately give them a refund and get your eBay and PayPal fees refunded. That way, you at least get something back. If you wait and eBay decides against you, then you lose all your fees.

Another area that can cause a lot of problems is people who claim to have received only one item when you have sent two or more items that they have purchased. There is truth in the saying 'experience is a teacher'. I have been forced to develop a coding system that I use on every order with more than one item. The system has significantly reduced the number of claims although there is still the occasional claim. It wastes a lot of time to resolve. On receiving such a claim, ask for a photograph of the envelope. If you have made a mistake, then the photograph of the envelope comes back almost instantly. If not, it goes very quiet. The brazen ones will claim to have put the envelope into the rubbish. However, it's human nature that if you receive an item that is incorrect, you put it back into the envelope and keep it not throw it away. If you do however make a mistake, it is better to apologise to the customer and come to an agreement on how to resolve the problem. It would be interesting to know how the same eBay customer would behave in a face to face environment in a shop.

I sell worldwide and because of this I receive many emails in different languages. When you find yourself in this situation use 'Google Translate' to translate the message. When you reply to the email, make sure to put the translated message at the top of your reply and include the message in your native tongue under the translated message. It makes solving problems with eBay and working out what you replied easier. Plus, you are not struggling to work out what you wrote before.

A lot of people will try to bully you on eBay. As the following case studies will demonstrate.

- I received an email from a buyer who I had sent three items to claiming that they had received two of what they had ordered, and one wrong item. The wrong item that they claimed I had sent was something I did not stock. I replied asking for a photograph, in return I got all sorts of abuse back plus being told that I was unprofessional for sending an incorrect item. I continued to ask for a photograph. They replied, "Please send me your email address so that I can send the picture." As most sellers know, eBay has banned the sending of email addresses by eBay messages. I replied that they could attach the photograph to their reply message. I also provided a description of where the 'attach button' was for the photograph. The reply came back, "This function is not on my eBay account." The reality is, this function is on every eBay account worldwide. But when confronted with such a customer you instantly know that there is something wrong here. I reported the buyer to eBay and used the report function to report them as well. I heard nothing else back.

- One buyer sent an email to me claiming that "my stock was full of fakes". They wanted a refund, and they were not going to send the item back again. Needless to say, it was a strange request for someone who wants to keep fake stock. I replied to them, and they sent another email demanding a refund. They reiterated that they were not going to send the stock back and if I did not refund them, they were going to give me negative feedback informing everyone that "I was selling fake products" so they claimed. In addition they were going to open a case against me. In eBay terms this is called 'feedback extortion'. I contacted eBay and worked out the best way to resolve this over the years. I have learned through experience that eBay can't do very much about the threat of negative feedback until it is given. However, having read the email they agreed that it was blackmail. I replied to the buyer and received yet a longer threatening email. At first, when you experience this, it is quite unsettling, but you start to get used to it. It's called bullying, and it's amazing how people can write such a forceful email. It would seem that some people get a thrill out of this and you just have to learn how to deal with the public.

- One person phoned me from a foreign country while I was on a train. I had no idea who they were, but they asked me about their order. I like to look after customers, but sometimes you just cannot remember everyone especially if you do not have access to a computer and can't access their information. I wrote down the eBay user id. Later, I thought I had resolved the problem by sending their order. Next thing I know, I received an email from this person complaining that I had not phoned them back. If I had phoned them during my day, it would have been in the middle of the night in their country and I doubt they would have been pleased to be woken up. I wrote back explaining this and got more abuse back. They complained in their email about everything imaginable, and all this time their order was in transit. Once they had received their order, they gave me negative feedback. I have absolutely no idea what their problem was or how I could have resolved it. Except that some people are never satisfied.

A word of advice, you have to work with customers to understand what is going on. Then use common sense and eBay support to resolve situations when they occur. But no matter what abuse you receive, never get angry and always be polite as it is very easy to get wound up. This is exactly what eBay customers expect. The aim is to upset the seller so that they respond in an angry mood. That way they get a licence to give you a damning feedback to put off other customers.

One Customer sent an email stating that their order had not arrived. I sent a reply and waited. Back came the usual email:

"The address is correct and it's not at the distribution office."
I asked what the address of the distribution office was. Back
came the reply, that stated a town. I reminded the customer
that I was trying to help and asked them to please supply the
exact address. Back came the reply again, this time with an
address and a threat of being reported to eBay. I contacted
Royal Mail the next day and it transpires that they had given
the wrong address again. Again, in situations like these, it's
hard to believe the Customer. They've already lied to you,
all they had to say was that the office was too far away and
they couldn't get to it - but instead they chose to lie. The
next e-mail arrived stating, "It's not arrived and I am going
to contact eBay." I spoke to eBay about this, and I agreed
that I would report them to Trust and Safety. In the end I
decided that I would send them a replacement item. I sent
an email to the Customer informing them that I was going to
send them a replacement item. Back came the reply, "You
do not need to bother I have bought a replacement." It is
likely that they received their item, and they did not want
another one. I sent the replacement anyway so that they
could not claim that they did not receive their item. Plus it
went by registered post so there could be no arguments
about not receiving it.

To put your mind at rest, the problems that I get are on
average less than 1% of all my sales. So it is not doom and
gloom as the majority of customers are totally honest.
Occasionally a Customer will contact me acknowledging
that they had received their order which had previously not
arrived. The other nice thing is the number of buyers who
receive refunds and then write back to me saying that their
order has arrived and ask to pay me back the refund. These
customers tend to restore my faith.

It is also true that sometimes for whatever reason that mail does not reach its destination within the estimated time frame. When a customer expects their order within that time frame they begin to feel frustrated. Such a problem is addressed through excellent customer service. Unfortunately there are buyers who set out to buy things off of eBay with their own agenda to obtain free items. You have to learn to deal with them in a professional manner.

An example of this is a case that was opened stating that I had addressed the item incorrectly since it has not been delivered. It is therefore my fault for not having the item delivered. The postal service has attempted to deliver the item but the address is not correct. Having just tried the address in Google Maps the address they have provided is incorrect. But they want a refund since they are claiming that I used the wrong address.

8

Negative, Neutral and Positive Feedback

The subject of Negative Feedback could fill another book. It is a fascinating subject. Feedback is the method that customers use to share their experience on eBay and your service and products. I was invited by eBay to take part in a Group Discussion about eBay. Six of us turned up, no one knew each other and we have never met again since. But it was fascinating when the discussion turned to Negative Feedback because every one of us had the same experiences. The person who was facilitating the event was amazed at what was being discussed and what buyers get up to. There were plenty of comments like, "You have got to be joking." There was a big debate, calling to permit sellers to give buyers negative feedback. While it would be fully justified in some cases, but it would put a lot of companies out of business.

There are a lot of tricks that buyers use with negative feedback. They use certain words that kill your business. EBay has a process for taking off defamatory comments but leaving the feedback on. If you provide a good service, you should have next to no problems with negative feedback. But it's something that you will still receive. For instance, if you agree to provide a refund, just do it. Do not wait until the customer has written to you three times. If you make a mistake, apologise. Just doing simple things like this go a long way to mitigate negative feedback.

When you receive negative feedback, the first thing to do is to reply to the customer. Be very polite, even though you may be angry. Reply with a saying like, "Thank you for your feedback ..." Everyone reads feedback, so do not use phrases like "The buyer lied," "This is rubbish," "Beware of this buyer," or my favourite, "You little liar ..." It makes your potential customers wary of you, and you may see a drop in sales. Being polite and not being confrontational is very important. It lets other buyers see you in a professional light. In fact, showing that you can deal with feedback often means you receive more sales.

The worst feedback is neutral feedback that says, "Great Sale," but is scored as neutral. Do the same things again, and thank them for the feedback when you reply.

Once you receive negative or neutral feedback, contact the buyer to find out what the problem is don't just take it and leave it on your record. Whatever you do, remember the golden rule - be polite. You may have an unhappy customer, someone trying to wreck your business or someone who does not know how feedback works. Thank them for their valuable feedback and inquire about the problem. This will normally calm down irate customers and in return you may receive a calm reply. That said experience has shown that very few customers reply to emails asking about negative or neutral feedback. Once you have contacted the customer, contact eBay since pre-emptively you have done what the eBay representative will ask you to do anyway.

Your aim is to get the negative or neutral feedback removed. Again be polite and do not get frustrated or shout, although you'll certainly feel like doing so. When I first started I would get really hyped up with eBay Customer Service. There are certain feedbacks that eBay will not remove. But if the text is rude, abusive, or has a link to a website it will be taken off – eBay is fair that way

One customer left me a negative feedback stating, "The customer service is **** and never helps anyone." I was shocked, but it was removed instantly. Another time, I received a negative feedback and contacted eBay. This customer had left ten negative feedbacks from their account, they had given a negative feedback to everyone who they had bought from. It was obvious that they had set up an eBay account with a motive in mind.

If eBay asks you to keep on trying to contact the buyer, I recommend you contact them another four times or so. Then get back to eBay again to get the feedback removed. They may or may not follow through, but being polite at all times is so important. When you phone eBay support, ask the person that answers the telephone how they are. Hardly anyone does this, and doing it will help to put them in a good mood, making them more likely to help you.

I have had some very interesting negative feedbacks over the years. I used to check when processing orders to ensure that the eBay and Pay addresses are the same. If the addresses did not correspond then I would contact the customer for confirmation of the correct shipping address. One particular customer had replied to my email about having a different address with a reply of, "Where is my item?" I wrote back again, stating that I did not know what address to use. After waiting for another two weeks, back came the reply, "Where is my item?" I replied again.

This time I received negative feedback stating, "Have not received item and Seller never replies to my questions." I, of course, as described above replied to the feedback, thanking them for the feedback. I contacted eBay. After explaining the circumstances, the negative feedback was removed. The customer sent their correct address details, and I posted their order making sure it was sent tracked to avoid further confusion or misunderstanding. What was intriguing was that the customer continually asked about the status of their order. This goes to show you that for some customers no matter how much you go out of your way, they are difficult to please.

I had a spate of negative feedbacks that made no sense at all. They kept on appearing on eBay, and there was no reason for them. Worse of all I was told by eBay that they would not remove the negative feedback because of the words they contained. Out of utter frustration, I contacted other sellers who had sold items to this customer. Only to discover that they had had the same experience with this particular customer. After investigative research, I discovered that this customer was selling the same items as me. They were buying items from all UK sellers to give them negative feedback - what a surprise. Once I contacted eBay and explained what I had done and the proof I had, the negative feedbacks was removed. The lesson from this is, once you have built a good reputation on eBay you can become a target to those competitors whose aim is to shut down your business.

The technique of contacting other sellers is very powerful. I have solved problems that I have had with buyers who were claiming that they had not had their orders delivered, only to discover they were doing this to everyone. I often contact other sellers and they contact me. Then use the evidence to put your case to eBay.

Whenever you suspect that you are about to receive a negative feedback, contact eBay Support and discuss the case with them in advance. In my experience, it is always easy to spot potential troublesome customers and eBay are always great for advice about how to avoid negative feedback.

If you enclose flyers in your orders, always add a note requesting that the customer contacts you before giving any negative feedback. As a reminder make sure that you save all your relevant email conversations using eBay messages, so that you have a record of any conversations that have taken place. Armed with a factual trail of evidence, eBay is likely to look at your case favourably as long as you talk to them politely.

When a customer has given you negative feedback, make contact with them and sort out their problem to the best of your ability. There are two advantages to this. First, if you do a good job and make them satisfied with what you have done for them, you're able to bring up the subject of removing the negative feedback. They may ignore you, but if you show that you care, they may well remove the negative feedback on their own. Second, if you do something wrong, people have a habit of telling everyone. If you solve their problem, they will give you a good report, and more people may buy from you through word of mouth. This is still the best marketing tool even with social media.

I do have an interesting dilemma on how to deal with customers that do not tell the truth. One example was a customer who claimed that they worked in an office that was open 24 hours a day. They raised a case against me, claiming that they had not received their order. They kept going on about their office being open 24 hours a day. I phoned the office in the evening it was shut. Then I had a case opened saying that they had not received their order. I replied to them and received a response that they had been to the Distribution Office on Friday. I wrote back and said that it was shut on Friday due to it being Good Friday. Back came the reply that they went on Thursday. I replied that the conversation had taken place on Friday—why would they have gone on Thursday if they hadn't spoken with me yet? In these two cases customers were not telling the truth, so why should I believe them? When I contacted eBay, they had the view that because the customer did not receive their order it did not seem to matter, and they could have made a mistake. I have a different view however that when someone lies once, they're unlikely to tell the truth next time.

There is a function on eBay to report a buyer. Use this where necessary as it goes direct to Trust and Safety. This department monitors all users and notes how many cases they have opened. You will find that eBay will send you an email saying that a buyer is no longer on eBay after they have been reported and seen not to be a good eBayer. Your rating is adjusted monthly by eBay after all the reports are submitted. So it's worthwhile just getting in touch whenever you have a problem with a customer.

The obvious step, of course, is to always block a customer whenever you receive a negative feedback. Otherwise, they may come back and give you another negative feedback.

If you are dealing with a person who has given you a neutral or negative feedback about a problem with the item and they are in contact with you, ask them what the condition of the item is that they provided the bad feedback for. If they reply that there is no problem with it, contact eBay and get the feedback removed.

Sometimes when eBay agrees to remove a feedback their system does not work properly. The feedback is not removed. Just get back to them until its removed.

At this point, I have spoken mainly about negative and neutral feedback. I should not forget the most important part of eBay: Positive Feedback. There will always be some people out to give you a bad critique. However, you should never forget the people who provide positive feedback. They are what keeps your account going and help support your business. Feedbacks like "Awesome," "Brilliant communicator," and "Fast Delivery," are what makes people come back and buy again. Your aim is to make everyone who buys from your eBay business have a great experience and to provide you with great feedback in return. This builds up your reputation.

9

Postal Provider

To have a successful online business requires you to use an efficient postal provider to deliver your mail. For Royal Mail, you require an Online Business Account to make it cost effective. Opening an account is easy, and it is up and running very quickly.

You may be sending the most delicate items, and you can plaster your packages with "Handle With Care" stickers as much as you like, but all postal providers totally ignore every sticker and will throw your parcel around with no care. Remember this when you are wrapping your orders.

You have to ensure that each order is carefully packaged to sustain rough handling. The envelope or wrapping has to be of a high standard and use a coloured tape since it is easy for your customer to see. Have you ever tried to open a parcel with see through tape? Ensure that there are no areas of the envelope that can get caught in any machinery. For instance, on closing the envelope flap put tape on both sides to avoid the envelope or parcel being caught in a conveyor belt. If the parcel is damaged in transit, it is unlikely to be put back together and sent on. In most cases it will just be lost and you will not be contacted. That said, there was one incident I was contacted one evening by my Postal Provider. A kind employee informed me that my parcel had been damaged. They carefully put it back together again and sent it on its way. But this does not happen often.

When I first started, I applied no tape externally to the envelope, and my orders were not reaching their destinations. Once I started adding tape to the envelopes, the losses declined. So my advice is to use tape. You have a far better chance of your order being delivered successfully.

The biggest adventure with Royal Mail was when they sent all of my parcels to Austria instead of Australia. I constantly contacted Royal Mail given the number of emails I was receiving from Customers. They denied all responsibility until one day I received a phone call from a Royal Mail employee. They informed me that it was the fault of British Airways because they had been using staff that could not speak English. I had to contend with an avalanche of emails to deal with from annoyed customers. Despite this, Royal Mail did not agree to any compensation, claiming the orders were arriving within 28 working days as per their policy. They later claimed that it never happened. Meanwhile I had customers in Australia asking why their order had arrived via Austria.

My greatest crisis was when Royal Mail decided to stop allowing a particular product to be shipped by air mail as it was regarded to be dangerous cargo since it was flammable. This was introduced by the airlines in conjunction with the mailing companies. I was blissfully unaware of this until a large number of overseas orders failed to reach their destination. I had initially assumed that the orders were getting lost. To my horror, I received a letter from Royal Mail listing the parcels that they had destroyed containing my products. I rang Royal Mail and asked what was going on since I knew nothing about this new rule. What transpired was that Royal Mail had sent out emails to every supplier of the product in the UK. But the correspondence had only been sent to companies that had a particular key word in their email address. My email address did not contain the key word, so I was ignored. They claimed there were posters in every Post Office, warning about these new rules. I do go to the Post Office regularly, but I had not seen any posters. Royal Mail explained that every parcel was being x-rayed. Any parcel that contained the product in question or an illegal substance was sent to Belfast to be checked and destroyed.

For the next delivery, I went to the Post Office and asked about the new rules on posting illegal substances. The person behind the counter knew nothing about it. I checked everywhere, and there was no sign of these mysterious posters anywhere. I rang the help desk again and was informed that the posters were up everywhere. Next visit to the Post Office, there was nothing yet again. Eventually after two weeks of checking, I found a small box in the corner of the Post Office full of posters warning about the new illegal substances. Another scenario is when I posted an order to Amsterdam with 20 items. It was sent by registered mail, however to my surprise it was never scanned into the system. The complete parcel vanished without any trace. Worse of all Royal Mail denied all responsibility. I lost hundreds of pounds worth of stock in this encounter with Royal Mail, and they refused to refund me for any of it. All this because they made sending these substances illegal but never bothered telling people about it.

The list that I received from Royal Mail of the total items destroyed was one tenth of what I lost. Even now, I still find orders mysteriously disappearing when being sent to destinations in the UK. As a result of this, I learned that whenever you make a complaint to your postal provider, you should ask for a reference number. Record it and keep on phoning up until they sort it out. If not, they will ignore you and do nothing about it. So the onus is on you to keep on top of your problem.

In 2014, after the privatisation of Royal Mail, I phoned up in mid-March to ask what the new prices would be. I was assured that the finance department would contact me. It took another seven phone calls to obtain the new prices. In addition I was also given wrong codes to use in the Online Business Account. I am not sure how incompetent a large service can be. However it's important to note that the majority of time Royal Mail is very good and helpful.

One thing to beware of when you send registered mail is that if Royal Mail forgets to scan your item into the system the item will not be tracked until it reaches another scanning facility. This upsets customers who have paid for a tracked parcel as they are unable to track their order. The most frustrating thing is when you enquire with Royal Mail, the voice on the end of the telephone would often inform you that you cannot claim for the parcel for 28 days – this is not helpful. Then, of course, you remember my favourite phrase: "We are very sorry." Which is used all the time.

The other thing to beware of are the customers who have not paid for a tracked service but then asks for the tracking number. An example is when a customer informs you that their order is not tracked, as they expect it to be. How they expect this to appear, I have no idea. They claim that their Post Office needs the tracking number to find their order.

When as a matter of fact the Post Office does not require the tracking number in order for them to receive their item as it was posted by standard post.

Whenever a customer claims to have not received their order, ask them to go to the Delivery Office to collect it. I have experienced customers who refuse to go to the delivery office but instead, go to the Post Office. The Post Office would then advice the customer that all parcels have been delivered. However the post person may or may not have left a card through the customer's door. But if the customer goes to the Delivery Office to collect their undelivered order in the first place. The problem would be solved.

As a business you can take your mail bags to the Post Office. Since you are a priority customer you can jump the queue and enjoy the stares of the general public waiting to be served. However, make sure that your mail bags are taken into the secure area of the Post Office before leaving. Do not leave them where any one can pick up your mail bags. You may have £1000 worth of goods in that mailbag or more. If someone steals it, it becomes your responsibility. Royal Mail will not accept any responsibility. A word of caution: when Royal Mail staff asks you just to leave your bags and they will collect them later, insist that they move your bags into the secure area of the Post Office.

10

Dealing With eBay

"Good morning. Thank you for calling eBay Customer Support. Please enter the code that you see displayed. If no code is available, please enter 1 ... We were able to recognise you."

How many times have you heard these words? The part I do not like is waiting 25 minutes to speak to an "agent" (which makes them sound like spies). I usually enjoy speaking to the eBay agents as most of them are very polite and very helpful. Always make sure to ask how they are when you first speak to them, no matter how pressing your matter is. Remember, they are human too. They have to listen to all our tales of woe, and if you can have a bit of social chat first, it makes them relax, and they are more likely to go a little bit further for you. You would be surprised at how far being polite can take you.

It's interesting that under certain circumstances the buyer can do no wrong. I have had buyers not telling the truth to me, only to be informed that people make mistakes. Some mistakes however are actually just lies. What do you do when someone starts telling you stories, and they are claiming that they have not received their order? What do you think? I know what I think.

The eBay contact centre is very good. The majority of the employees are very helpful and know what they are talking about. They provide good advice and assistance to very frustrated and angry sellers and customers but they know how to remain calm and polite. When you ask how they are you are one in a million.

If you chat with them nicely, you will get many hints that will help you with your business. I have had lots of hints to help me, and I have shared with them how I deal with certain situations which I am sure they pass on to other eBay sellers. Overall, it's a very good service that helps you a lot. Your best bet is to avoid getting angry with the staff; they are only there to assist you. It helps greatly with your relationship with eBay. Remember to give—do not always take.

Treat eBay Customer Support as part of your team. Even though it's only you, they will assist you with your plight. When you ring them, be courteous as they have to look up your records and read your emails. No matter how fast their super computers are this takes time to do - so be patient.

You sometimes get transferred to the US eBay office when it is busy in your local office. When you are speaking about things that are eBay related that will be no problem. But they will not be aware of local services that you have. For instance I had a problem with a mail issue that people from the US did not understand.

11

Positive Attitude

Positive attitude is one of the most powerful tools when it comes to starting a business, e-commerce or otherwise. After all, you have to believe in yourself to succeed. How many millions of people do you see heading to work in the morning for the daily grind? They arrive at work, get stressed all day doing their best for their company, come home at night they sit down in front of the television until they eventually go to bed. They get up the next morning, only to do the same thing again. Others bring work home and have little balance between their work and personal lives. They are tiny cogs in the huge engine that is the modern workforce. If they are no longer needed, they are removed replaced. New technology that was forecast for the 1990s is now being introduced and taking over people's jobs.

I started work at 15 years old in the Royal Air Force. Some of my experiences that I had were challenging and I wish that I had known about having a positive mind-set.

Knowing how to manage teams, deal with people and stay positive at the same time is vital, and I can give you several examples where I went through bad experiences and wish I had been more positive. I was given my appraisal by one of my managers, and I knew that they did not like me. My appraisal was glowing, apart from this tiny thing that I had supposedly done. Due to this, I was marked down.

I have managed many teams, and all of my teams know what I want from them. I work with them and support them. Doing this builds up mutual respect between the employee and the manager. If someone doesn't understand a task, you explain it to him or her. I can recall the number of times I have spoken about various topics or given presentations on a subject. At the end of my presentation, I always ask, "Do you understand this?" I would receive a chorus of "Yes," from the audience. When I pressed and reassured them that I wanted to be sure they truly understood it was only then that people spoke up.

I gave a presentation to a group of people who made displays for a product that I worked on, related to Air Traffic Control (ATC). I watched as the marketing person gave their presentation and was struck by blank looks and no questions. During the break, I spoke to the head of the organisation and asked what the problem was. They said, "No one understands what you are talking about. You use all this ATC jargon, and it just does not make any sense to any of us."

When I present to an audience I enjoy audience participation. Instead of giving my planned presentation I changed it to use examples of what people understood. Instead of talking about a flight plan being logged and using all the different support functions for Air Traffic Control. I spoke about the similarity to catching a bus to go to the pub. The bus turning up late being similar to a delayed flight. I shouted at the audience and woke them up and got them participating. I had lots of questions about how it all worked since they finally understood what I was talking about. The marketing person was not happy with me, but I had the audience eating out of my hand and was enjoying myself. The person in charge extended my 30-minute talk to an hour. I was thanked many times afterwards for such an excellent presentation. The art of learning is not to teach someone something but it is to explain how something is similar to something that they know. I talked about buses because everyone understands about a bus, but not everyone understands Air Traffic Control.

The industries I worked in had a knack for finding out who was irresponsible then give them a promotion. One day I walked into my Manager's office and asked, "What do I have to break to get promoted." I received a blank look from my Manager and their sidekick. I said, Well, to get promoted one has to do something wrong. I must be doing okay because you have never promoted me." They just laughed. I went out, found another job, and put the offer on my Manager's desk. I told him, either you promote me or I am leaving. As if by magic, I was suddenly promoted. It is terrible that you have to go to such lengths to get ahead in the corporate world.

I had always had a job since I was 15, and I paid my stamp every month to successive governments. But, I was made redundant. It was probably one of the worst experiences of my life. It was announced one sunny morning that the government had terminated the contract that I was working on, effective at 11 a.m. There was no compassion or empathy. It was just another announcement. This contract was about to deliver a very powerful solution to an age-old problem in the country. But it was cancelled, and there was nothing anyone could do about it. We all went home and were told to be in at 10 o'clock the next morning. We gathered in Human Resources (also nicknamed Human Remains) to be briefed by a director. The first four words were announced with a smile on his face, "There will be redundancies." This is the worse way to make anyone redundant. They don't care. The effect on me was devastating; I could not believe it. I had worked all these years, and everything I had done was gone.

All the meetings started about going through the redundancy process. It was horrible, easily the worst experience of my life. This director was callous. I recall going to "Human Remains" to get some information but due to my level of stress accidently went to the wrong room and walked into his office by mistake. He just treated me like dirt, shouting at me that I had come into the wrong room. At one of our meetings, someone said: "The Government cancelled the contract, and the company just dumped its employees and walked away." They were absolutely right. This is the way that a big corporation treats people who have families, mortgages, and have been loyal to them by working hard and trying their best. You become nobody at the drop of a hat. People with brilliant minds were talking about becoming bus drivers. I remember asking for a recruitment event to be organised to help people find other employment, which was actually acted upon. Nonetheless, we were given an early pay-off and let go. The government never announced the termination of the contract, so really no one knew about it. I always laugh to myself when I hear politicians complaining about the problem that this would have solved. Governments make decisions and evade questions or omit details to get away with everything.

When I hear about people being made redundant on the news, I really feel for them. Having been through the experience, I know what it feels like now. It is horrible, and I would not wish it on my worst enemy. In our case, the company only issued around 90 redundancies. I remember David Cameron being interviewed on TV about coal mines being closed and talking about giving money to help. The commentator asked, "You are giving money to keep the mines open?" "Oh, yes," replied David. Three weeks later, it was announced that the government was to give ten million pounds to aid with redundancies. Following my redundancy I went to the job centre to sign on. Only to learn that governments should learn how to treat people. My Curriculum Vitae was reviewed, and it was obvious that the person who read it didn't understand my experience. They went to their computer, checked a few things, and asked, "Do you fix televisions?" After a few weeks of signing on, I had to attend a big meeting in the job centre during which everyone who attended was in my position were told that we had to apply for jobs. The vacancy list I was presented with was barman, shelf stocker, and cashier. When I asked if they had any vacancies for engineering, there was complete silence. I was informed that they would get back to me. But no one ever did. I do not blame the job centre staff. I blame the government for having no idea how to manage educated people.

After I was made redundant, I started my eBay business properly and I began to build an infrastructure for the business. But every so often, I would get angry, sad, and happy all at once about being made redundant. The mood swings were awful, and I could not control them. After two months reality kicked in, I settled down and began to work better. I wish I had understood more about a positive mindset then as it would have helped me greatly.

Being positive has a great effect on your life. When things go wrong, don't point the finger and blame people. Instead, work out a solution to the problem. It's easy to say it, but it's harder to do. Nonetheless, what has happened is in the past, and there is no point in bringing it back up again.

I have only just started to work this way, and it's having a huge impact on my life. At the end of 2013, I did some work for someone who believes they have celebrity status (the term, I believe, is a wannabe). I worked 120 hours in 10 days. It was incredibly hard, but I delivered the results. I was given a cheque for a substantial amount of money as compensation for my efforts. They contacted me the next day and said that they could not afford to pay me a lump sum and that they would pay me in two instalments. I agreed not to cash the cheque. Lo and behold, they never paid me. This caused my family great hardship since I had dropped everything to make this project work. So I found myself short of money. To make it worse, the same client contacted me the next year to ask me to go to New York while they still owed me money. Once I found the strength to overcome this and push it to the back of my mind, things began to improve.

Lots of people talk about the mental game and people rubbish it, but it's actually true. Keep a positive mental attitude and aim for your goal. Keep thinking about your dream. Create a book or PowerPoint that shows what you want to be or the lifestyle you want to have, and keep looking at it.

I recently listened to a video about meditation. Your mind is a very powerful thing and having experienced mood swings, you start to understand how disruptive an unfocused mind can be to your work. I have found that sitting quietly for ten minutes and concentrating on one of my dreams is a wonderful experience. It empties your mind of the daily noise around you and makes you feel refreshed.

People have asked about eBay, and I have provided them with courses about how to make eBay work for them. They often become worried about the amount of effort it takes to set up an eBay business and get it working. I started at the beginning and built up my knowledge of eBay. You have to learn new skills, and you face challenges every day. But you have to overcome these challenges and keep on learning.

I recently spoke to a relative of mine who is leaving Primary School and going to Secondary School. They have to take a series of tests, which they are worried about. You can imagine how much pressure a young person feels. The school wants good results since it provides better statistics for the school and probably attracts more money and pupils. Parents want their children to do their best. The advice I gave them was to relax and avoid worrying. Practice for the tests, and your confidence will increase. Keep practising the skills you are the weakest at. Then practice the ones you are best at, to reassert your confidence. When you sit the exams, answer the questions that you find easy first. As your confidence increases go back to the ones that you skipped. Work your way through the test, and do the best you can. They passed with flying colours.

Setting up your own business is the same. It takes dedication, practice and hard work. You will be under pressure. But do the bits that you find easy first. For eBay, create an account and link it to PayPal. Then start playing with eBay. Look around and find out how it works. Practice putting an item on and adjust the wording until you are happy with it. Then put it online. This is your starting point. Keep working on the areas that you find easy until you gain confidence and can go back to the areas that you find challenging.

One of my examples is the time I mastered how to put variations on to eBay. It took a bit of working out. But it is far easier than listing all the variations in the description and managing them manually. Now, someone buys one item and I receive an email informing me which variation they purchased. There is no manually updating of the description, forgetting to manage the inventory and running out of stock to worry about (leading to upset customers). It's really simple now.

There are so many references out there that offer advice about how to do things. In reality, to be a success you have to work at it. Nothing in this world comes for free; there is always a cost in time and/or money. Find yourself a niche and work at it. You have to love your products. For eBay, people who look at your products and ask questions need replies. You must have expert knowledge of your products. But find a niche that interests you (and isn't saturated) then work to master it. Now you have a rare, highly marketable skill. I am an expert in requirements and testing. A lot of what I have learnt in these skills I use in my eBay business and can command a fee for. The majority of people do not understand requirements while I find it very easy and can picture a complete system in my head. This all came about while I worked on a project where the leader ran out of ideas. I offered to take over and started to run the group and work on requirements. Kept on learning every day and never looked back.

I have gradually built up my expertise in eBay, but it has taken time and dedication to do it. I spend an hour every day educating myself. I have audio books, printed books and videos running in the background when I am working. These moments of education have made me a better person and help me to become more determined to succeed.

As Dr John Demartini said, "Dedicate your life to a cause that inspires you and also greatly serves others. Master Plan your life. If you don't fill your day with high priorities, it will automatically become filled with low priorities".

12

Using Your Expertise

Consultancy is a way of assisting eBay customers. As an eBay expert, I have had people contacting me asking for assistance. I have built up a good rapport with eBay and had enquiries about many things. I have had requests from all sorts of people. From individuals wanting me sell stuff they could not sell themselves, to charities and organisations wanting me to put on lectures. One of the strangest things I have been asked about is selling beautiful, handmade costumes.

I have been contacted about things which have not sold and being thrown off of eBay. It has been an interesting experience. I have attempted to sell things on eBay that are unusual some which I have successfully sold some I have not. I have tried to promote services like massage, but it has not been successful at all. I have had some enquiries but no sales. But if you do not try, you will never know.

One thing to remember and this is very important. You can contact me about a problem on eBay, and I can give advice to you. For instance I was contacted by a charity about a problem they had. It was a great opportunity—the charity had helped unemployed people to start running their own businesses. I sorted out the problem and shared some advice. But when it came to speaking to eBay to resolve the matter only the account owner can speak to eBay. I found out all the likely scenarios and worked out the best way forward. But the account owner had to make the final phone call.

I sold two three-piece suites, which amazed me. They were collected from the owner. Even although you clearly state that they have to be collected from a certain area you still receive questions about you transporting them for free to their residence hundreds of miles away. The most amusing things I sold were weights and weight training apparatuses. I was asked to come to the owner's house to see if I could sell their weights. I agreed to do it. When I arrived, I went down into the basement to take a photograph of the first set of weights then returned to the second floor, putting the first set on eBay. I went back downstairs to take the next photograph. As I did, my mobile rang, and it was a potential buyer wanting to buy the first set of weights. They were on eBay for five minutes and sold. The customer came around, paid with cash, and the weights were gone. The weights sold amazingly well; I was stunned at their popularity. They were picked up from the owner so quickly, and the people buying them were so polite.

I receive lots of questions, such as "Will this sell on eBay?" That is the million-dollar question. I can do the marketing for you and give advice on the best price. But it's all down to solving people's problems. If what you are selling is solving a problem, it will sell.

The answer to the million dollar question "WHAT DO I SELL ON EBAY" Is Sell what is selling well now.

13

Digital Marketing and eBay

Digital marketing is an amazingly powerful method for selling on the Internet. However, while you are selling on eBay, you can use the same techniques to build up your list of potential buyers. After all, eBay is a very popular ecommerce platform that is used worldwide. You can sell literally anything on eBay, from a pair of socks to an aircraft. I could not believe it when I read about someone buying a Harrier Jump Jet on eBay. The range of what is available is amazing. As an example out of research curiosity I entered jet aircraft into the eBay search engine. What came up was "English Electric Lightning P1B RAF Aircraft Rolls Royce Avon Mk209 Jet Engine" for sale only £29,999. As I said it's amazing what you can find. It has 183 watchers.

Once you get yourself set up as a business on eBay and start selling. First, you start selling simple things and then gradually the range that you sell starts to expand. The next stage is to open a shop on eBay. This gives your goods on eBay more focus since your potential customers can go and browse in your shop, making your complete range of stock far more accessible to your customers. I found that people started purchasing my stock in threes and fours. I regularly sell ten of an item. However, you have to be careful of people wanting deals. Get them to do the work of stating what they want and estimating a cost. Too many times, I have created a list of items and prices, and sent it off only to receive no reply.

If your customers are willing to purchase ten of your stock in one transaction, it shows the level of trust that you have built up within your eBay business. But I can tell you creating this rapport is hard work. You must provide great service, reply to emails quickly, and work hard to maintain a high level of integrity within your business. The amount of feedback that you have is a good indication of how well your business is performing it boosts your confidence

Each person or company that buys from your eBay shop knows that they have done business with you and trusts you. You have created a relationship with that buyer, which you can use to your advantage. You haven't just provided them with an item from your eBay shop, but with great service, as well. The majority of people are happy, if not delighted, with your service.

When you are collecting your income into PayPal, you will have an accounting system that will move each piece of sale data to your accounting system. The accounting system has a function for downloading your customer details, including their name, address, and e-mail address. Once you have this data, get a free trial of a Customer Relationship Management (CRM) platform. I have tried out lots of different CRM software—some are very good, and some are not so good. Keep taking free trials until you find one that really works for you. Some CRM platforms I have found very difficult to use. Others are user-friendly and have a great support. It's about what works for you.

I eventually found a good CRM platform that I liked. It had great support and was relatively easy to use. I loaded in the data that I had downloaded from the accounting system, after formatting it correctly. Given the high number of buyers I have, and some of the formatting in the Comma Separated Variable (CSV) file that the system provided, formatting the data took quite a long time. When it was finished, I loaded the data into the CRM software, and I was ready to go.

First, I had to create an email to send out. The email started with a "thank you" for purchasing from me on eBay and provided a link to my eBay shop. It also provided a link to an item that I am promoting and a free article that I had written on the item. Your customers must, of course, have the ability to opt out from these messages.

I sent it out and, much to my chagrin, the CRM software did not send out the emails immediately. Instead, there was a delay of about three hours before sending. I knew it had finally gone out when the out of office messages started appearing, which just goes to show you how many eBay orders are placed in the office.

There were a few emails that came back from interested customers, wanting to know what they had bought. Even after a few weeks, I am still receiving responses about my email.

In general a eBay business can be for anyone who is serious and committed to making serious money whether full time or part time the choice is yours. However, like any business or service events in the global world have a knock on effect on eBay sales as buyers are sensitive to such events.

For example, when the USA and Russia started talks about the Ukraine, there was a significant downturn in sales on eBay. Everything quickly picked up again once things settled back down.

14

Employees

There is a saying that you should never forget. To make a fortune you have to work on your business not in it. To do this you need at least one employee to start with.

You may think employee? I can't afford that. But once you start to build up your orders, you will need help. Plus if you want to grow or expand your business you need to free yourself to be able to manage it efficiently and it is almost impossible for a one man band to do all the operations in business. You will want to go on holiday or have a night off then with an employee you can.

One of the first employees I had informed me that they were leaving due to a move of house. It was a real shame since they were amazing. I put an advert in a shop window at first. This seemed to be a wonderful place to advertise, but the candidates who phoned weren't great.

One of them wanted to start immediately, without sending a CV or interviewing. Another sent a CV that looked quite good, but when it came to an interview they never turned up. I then advertised on a website. I listed the region that I wanted people from since if you are working part-time. I preferred a local person as this is an evening part time post and I want my employee to be safe. I received CVs from recent graduates, some with poor grades, who could not find work.

The advert then started to generate some higher quality responses. There were some good people about. One lady I spoke to wanted to work for a month until moving to Nottingham. I had another application from a lady who lived close by. I interviewed them and they were fine. I interviewed another candidate who was very good. I invited both to come and see what I do. The first one did not appear however the second one arrived and seemed to be satisfactory. Since they were fresh from university I did expect them to have some common sense. But I was probably naïve.

They started on a Monday, which coincided with a very busy day. I worked through the orders with them, explaining how I did things. Then I asked them to take over under my supervision. I worked through a few items and, after getting the hang of what I do, they seemed to have a good idea of my process. The last thing I said was, "If you have any problems, please ask me. You don't need to struggle or make mistakes."

I started the process of packing. After five minutes, I went back to find them moving a page about and the mouse not working properly. They had got lost and had just carried on without asking.

After all the orders were processed, I introduced them to the fine art of packaging. In order to avoid mistakes I write a short code on the back of the address label to signify what to wrap. This seemed to cause them no end of problems.

Eventually, I got them wrapping. This was mad—I needed to have about eight arms to cope with making sure they were doing things correctly while I tried to handle other tasks as well. I finally let them go home when, after two hours, they started clock-watching. It then took about three hours to clear the mess they had created.

The next day had to be better. It brought a slight improvement. I got through the list of emails and then got them packing. I was still processing the emails while they started packing. My wife told me that they were making a complete mess of packing things. Then, they started asking where the labels were. That sounded like a disaster and it was. Shortly after, the clock-watching started again. I let them go home. This caused me a lot of hassle as I had to continue to work for the next two hours to clean up the mess. Plus I wrapped all the new orders that had come in.

It takes me about ten minutes to wrap six items (about 90 seconds per item), including adding the Customs label and tracking. Meanwhile, it was taking my new employee about seven minutes to wrap one item it was a disaster. The next two nights were similar, and by the end of the fourth night, I'd had enough. I made up my mind that they were not coming back. The last night they were with me, I ignored the clock-watching at 9pm and kept them working until 10pm. The level of clock-watching increased and became amusing around 9:30pm. By 9:45pm, it was purely comical. At 10pm, I let them go home. They vanished out the door faster than they had moved the rest of the evening.

When they arrived the next day, I explained that I had a problem and let them go. I do not like doing things like that, but I had to handle it for the good of my business. On Friday night, I processed the orders. They were finished faster than any other day that week—what a relief! The weekend was hard work but ended all right. The following week, the fallout began. The mistakes that they had made came back to haunt me. I have cleared them all up now, but this was a terrible experience.

Since then, I have raised my standards, and I expect other people to do the same thing. Raising your level of expectation has a tremendous effect on you. I promised myself then and there, to always set my standards high in the future. It makes you focus harder on what you need to do to make your business a success and same applies to choosing an employee.

15

Conclusion

It is true that building up a successful business requires a lot of hard work and sacrifices. Indeed this has been my experience. As my wife will often say there are three in this relationship and I come last. But she says it with good heart

This is a view of how I have worked on eBay and created a profitable business. It's often hard work and lots of people have spoken to me about how they lack time to make a business work. They want to spend more time with their family or take more vacations.

You can take the advice of the banker who has never run a small business in their life but claims to know how you should run your business. Or you can take my advice. I have received over 18000 feedbacks. I am using eBay every day I understand it. Presentations I have given about eBay have generated massive interest, simply because of my knowledge. I understand how eBay works and what it takes to make it work properly. This is not the key presses - it is the processes involved. I have been through just about every conceivable problem with eBay. From customers not receiving items, having someone hack into your account and listing their items, and more. I am still learning. Equally eBay also continues to evolve and implement changes to improve their system. Thus, if you read a book with eBay key presses, it would be out of date in about a month. That's why

I've created this Book—so that I can continue to update it to reflect the most current information. That is why there are no screen shots of eBay.

My advice is, if you want to try eBay, start small and try it out but it is not for everybody. After all, you must learn as a company how eBay works and what the potential problems are. So many businesses or individuals would be businesses or individuals on eBay but they fail due to their lack of know how. The main thing that makes your business is customer service. You have to be tough, but providing great service gives you the edge you need to make your eBay business as successful as mine.

The most important advice is, you have to make a profit. If you are not making a profit then your business will fail. No matter how many orders you have, you will lose money. As you have to factor in all your expenses into each item for sale. Some items are expensive to purchase and in a difficult market you may only make a small profit. But you have to make profit.

You should always remember it is not necessarily the price of your item that sells it. It is a combination of equally important factors that make up your unique selling point 'USP'. Quality, quick delivery, good customer service, reputation and last of all price.

I will never forget an Operations Director who gave me invaluable advice when I had just started. It's not the price that makes your business a success. It's what you do different to your competitors. Better known in theory as your unique selling point.

Now that I have shared my experiences. You need to go and practice the skills that I have described, required to make your eBay business a success. The rest is up to you. A saying I was taught a long time ago was JFDI – JUST ****** DO IT. If I can do this you can do it.

Congratulations on getting this far. Now that you have read the book. Get yourself on to eBay. Start selling. Sell anything just get the feel of what it is like at first. Start finding your niche to sell. You have to be passionate and know your niche. Then start to expand. If you have any questions ask me – I am here to help.

Email george@meetgeorgewallace.com